Basketball's
BIG MEN

Basketball's
BIG MEN

Richard Rainbolt

Lerner Publications Company
Minneapolis

ACKNOWLEDGMENTS

The illustrations are reproduced through the courtesy of: pp. 6, 42, 46, 61, 63, 66, 76, Vernon J. Biever; pp. 9, 12, 23, 26, 79, United Press International; p. 16, Philadelphia 76'ers; pp. 29, 33, Independent Picture Service; pp. 37, 40, 49, 53, Photography Incorporated; p. 56, John E. Biever; pp. 70, 72, 78, Milwaukee Bucks.

LIBRARY OF CONGRESS CATALOGING IN PUBLICATION DATA

Rainbolt, Richard.
Basketball's big men.

(The Sports Heroes Library)
SUMMARY: Brief biographies emphasizing the careers of ten basketball stars: George Mikan, Dolph Schayes, Bob Pettit, Bill Russell, Elgin Baylor, Jerry Lucas, Wilt Chamberlain, Willis Reed, Rick Barry, Kareem Abdul-Jabbar.

1. Basketball—Biography—Juvenile literature. [1. Basketball—Biography] I. Title.

GV884.A1R34 1975   796.32'3'0922[B][920]   74-27472
ISBN 0-8225-1054-5

Published simultaneously in Canada by
J. M. Dent & Sons (Canada) Ltd., Don Mills, Ontario

Manufactured in the United States of America

International Standard Book Number: 0-8225-1054-5
Library of Congress Catalog Card Number: 74-27472

Contents

Professional basketball is not like most other top American sports. It does not have a long history of superstars. In fact, it does not have a long history at all. Only in modern times—from about 1950 to the present—has the game become popular around the country.

One thing that has made basketball popular is the presence of the big men on the court. In pro basketball's early days, the players were seldom over 6 feet tall. As a result, the play was slow and the scores were low. But for the last 30 years, Americans have been growing taller and taller. And this has made for taller basketball players, many of them as fast as the smaller players of years before. With these big men on the court, basketball has changed a lot. The game has become faster, and the scores higher. Now, no one is surprised when a pro team scores 100 points or more.

Because these changes in basketball have come so quickly, most of the game's best players are still alive. In fact, many of them are still playing. This book tells the stories of 10 of the greatest big men in basketball. Each player was at least 6 feet, 5 inches tall. Some of them changed the game into what it is today—fast-moving, high-scoring, and physical. The others are keeping it that way.

All of the big men in this book were top college players before they became stars in the pro game. They range from the first of the giants, George Mikan, to such recent superstars as Rick Barry and Kareem Abdul-Jabbar. In height, they range from Wilt Chamberlain, who is 7-feet-2, down to Elgin Baylor, "only" 6-feet-5.

Now turn to the next page, and read the stories of how these big men made it to the top of the basketball world!

George Mikan (wearing glasses) struggles to keep the ball.

George Mikan

No other player has done more for basketball than George Mikan. The Babe Ruth of basketball, he was the first giant on the court. His great size and his great playing helped make basketball popular around the country. But before George Mikan became a superstar, he had to overcome many problems.

George Lawrence Mikan was born in Joliet, Illinois, in 1924. When he was a boy, no one dreamed he would ever become a top basketball player. Young Mikan was tall, but he was also slow and awkward. And because his eyesight was bad, he had to wear strong glasses. In high school, George was cut from the basketball team when his coach saw that he could not play without glasses. There had *never* been a good player who had worn glasses, said the coach.

In 1942, Mikan decided to go to DePaul University in Chicago. By this time, he was over 6-feet-6 and weighed more than 200 pounds. No one had ever coached him in basketball, but Mikan was set on playing. When the coach at DePaul saw George Mikan, he knew he could make a good player out of the giant. Glasses and all!

Under the coach, Mikan worked hard to improve his timing and to build up his strength and speed. He did this by jumping rope, doing push-ups, and running. Finally, the work paid off. In 1943, George Mikan made DePaul's first-string basketball team. Most people thought of him as a freak, for they had never seen a player of his size. And the experts said that he had no skill. The overgrown player with the glasses would never be any good, they laughed.

But George Mikan did not care what the "experts" said. He surprised them all by trying even harder. With long hours of practice, he learned how to throw the hook shot better than any other player in college basketball. Mikan's great shooting made his scores go up and up. By the end of his first season with DePaul, Mikan had become such a good player that he was named to the college basketball All-America team. Now, the crowds did not laugh when the giant came on the court. They cheered!

Mikan's last two seasons with DePaul were even better than his first one. He was the country's top scorer both seasons, averaging 23 points a game. And he was named to the All-America team two more times. In 1945, Mikan led his team to the National Invitation Tournament (NIT) in New York. He was hurt soon after the tournament began, but this did not stop him. In one of the last games, he scored 53 points—as much as *all the players* on

the other team had scored! DePaul won the NIT title, and Mikan won a place in the record books.

When he graduated in 1946, George Mikan was known all across the country. Professional basketball was struggling to stay alive then, and Mikan was the new blood it needed. Before long, he signed with the Chicago Gears of the National Basketball League (NBL). His salary was $60,000 —more than any other pro had ever gotten. But Mikan earned it by bringing new life to the NBL. Every place the giant played, large crowds turned out to see him. The Chicago Gears went broke in 1947, but pro basketball took hold in other cities.

12

And part of the reason for this was George Mikan. There were *always* more people at the games in which he played.

After the Gears went broke, Mikan joined another NBL team—the Minneapolis Lakers. George became the Lakers' star player, and the Lakers built one of pro basketball's greatest teams around him. In the 1947-48 season, Mikan led the Lakers to their first world championship. He was the top scorer in the NBL that season, averaging 21 points a game. And when the season ended, he was named the NBL's Most Valuable Player.

In 1948, Mikan and the Minneapolis Lakers left the NBL and joined a brand-new basketball league. This league became known as the National Basketball Association (NBA), and George Mikan became its first superstar. During the six years from 1948 to 1954, Mikan led the Minneapolis Lakers to *five* world championships! And for three straight seasons—1948-49, 1949-50, and 1950-51—he was the NBA's number-one scorer. Mikan averaged about 28 points a game during this time. He scored as many as 61 points in a single game, and he set a record for the most points scored in one season (1,932).

Not surprisingly, George Mikan became known as "Mr. Basketball." But if Mikan was successful, his success wore him down. The big man took a lot of physical punishment, for opposing teams had no other way to stop him. When Mikan planted his 6-foot-10, 245-pound body in front of the basket, the only way to score was to run into him or over him. Before his career was over, Mikan suffered two broken legs, three broken fingers, a broken wrist, and a broken nose. It took more than 150 stitches to close up all his wounds. But Mikan was strong, and he learned to play the game as roughly as other players. When he ran to the basket for a shot, his elbow led the way like a large cutting blade.

With his size, strength, and great hook shot, George Mikan made the Lakers an unbeatable team. To help give other teams a fair chance to win, the NBA made some new rules. Only one of these rules hurt Mikan's playing, and that one came toward the end of his career. The rule said that a team must shoot for a basket within 24 seconds of their getting the ball. If they did not, the ball would go to the other team. Mikan had always been slow in getting down the court to his position. And because he was usually guarded by two or three men, it took a long time to get the ball to him. So, by making the game faster, the 24-second rule made it harder for Mikan to score.

George Mikan stopped playing in 1954 so that he could become general manager of the Lakers. Two years later, he left professional basketball for good. Mikan had set many records during his years with the Lakers, including the one for the most points scored in a career. In eight years, he had scored a total of 11,764 points!

George Mikan was not only the first of the giants in pro basketball, but also one of the most popular. He was so highly thought of that he was named the "greatest basketball player from 1900 to 1950." The big man received an even greater honor in 1960, when he was named to the Basketball Hall of Fame. George Mikan now lives in Minneapolis, where he is a lawyer.

Dolph Schayes

Of all basketball's big men, Dolph Schayes had one of the longest careers. Like Lou Gehrig in baseball, Schayes became known as basketball's "Iron Man." He played 16 seasons with the Syracuse Nationals of the NBA. And he set a record by playing in 703 games in a row!

Dolph Schayes was born in New York City in 1928. As a boy, he showed little interest in sports. His father had been a boxer, and he wanted Dolph to be one, too. But Dolph did not like boxing. The boy was just too good natured for rough sports.

After he got a little older, Dolph finally found a sport he liked. That sport, of course, was basketball. Dolph tried out for the basketball team at DeWitt Clinton High School, and he made it. At first, however, he was not a very good player. Schayes was a tall, skinny boy who could shoot well, but who rarely got into the thick of play to grab the rebounds. When he *did* try for the rebounds, Dolph got knocked around by other, more rugged, players. He didn't mind, though. He just wanted to play the game, even if that meant getting pushed around.

After Schayes went to New York University (NYU), he became a better player. He still had trouble getting the rebounds, but his great shooting made him a high scorer. Soon, people started to take notice of him. When Schayes graduated from NYU in 1948, two professional teams asked him to play for them. The New York Knickerbockers offered him $6,000 a year. Then the Syracuse Nationals made a better offer, and Dolph took it. Schayes was to stay with the Nationals for all of his 16 years as a pro.

Dolph Schayes did not do very well during his first year with Syracuse. He averaged less than 13 points a game. And for a player who stood 6 feet, 8 inches tall, he did not grab nearly as many rebounds as he should have. But a long, hard talk with his coach changed all that. After the talk, Dolph started to fight for the rebounds. As his playing became rougher, he became one of the leading rebounders in pro basketball. Gone forever were the days when Dolph Schayes would let other players push him around!

In his second year with the Syracuse Nationals, Dolph led his team to the championship playoffs of the NBA. The Nationals lost the playoffs to the great George Mikan and his Minneapolis Lakers. But Dolph came back even stronger the next year. In the 1950-51 season, he won the NBA rebounding title by beating out George Mikan. This was one of the high points in Schayes's career.

Dolph Schayes had learned to do battle with other big men for the rebounds. He had also learned that when you play rough, you get hurt. In 1952, he broke his right wrist. This would have been a problem for most right-handed shooters, but it wasn't for Dolph Schayes. After the cast was put on his right hand, Schayes learned how to shoot with his *left hand!* Then he finished out the season, missing only three games. Dolph would not miss another game until many years later—after a string of 703 straight games.

In 1954, Schayes and the Syracuse Nationals had their best season ever. The Nationals won the 1954-55 NBA championship, and Dolph averaged 18.5 points a game. By this time, Schayes had become one of the most colorful players in the NBA. Every time he made a basket, he returned to the other end of the court with his arm over his head and his fist clenched. Dolph's victory signal became a familiar sight to fans all across the country.

Over the years, Schayes became known as the

most accurate shooter among all the big men in pro basketball. Other players, like Wilt Chamberlain and Kareem Abdul-Jabbar, had better scoring averages than Schayes. But most of their shots were made from close to the basket. Dolph Schayes was a good shooter not only from close in, but also from the outside. In addition, he was one of the most accurate free-throw shooters the game has ever known.

Before the start of the 1963-64 season, the Syracuse Nationals were moved to Philadelphia and renamed the Philadelphia 76ers. Dolph Schayes was made player-coach of the team. A short time later, he retired from playing so that he could coach full time. When he retired, Dolph took with him lifetime records in almost every category of pro basketball: games, rebounds, field goals, free throws, and points. The once-mild player had even set a record for personal fouls! He had become such a rough player that some experts said he was a complete team offense all by himself.

In the 1965-66 season, Dolph Schayes was named NBA Coach of the Year. His team won the NBA Eastern Division title that year. But it lost the championship playoffs to the Boston Celtics. After this happened, Dolph was fired by the owner of the 76ers. It was not enough that the 76ers had made a good finish. The team's owner felt that they should have won the championship. When they lost it, all the blame was put on Schayes.

Dolph Schayes hated to leave his team. He felt better, though, when he was named supervisor of officials for the NBA. With this job, Schayes was able to remain a part of the game he loved.

Dolph's playing days are over. But Dolph is remembered as the best long-term player in the history of the NBA. He played 1,035 games during his 16 seasons in pro basketball. And he was the first pro ever to score 15,000 points, or to come even close to 20,000 (his career total was 19,249). Dolph's scoring records have since been passed by Wilt Chamberlain and other great players. But in his own day, no one ever came close to playing as well as Dolph Schayes. In 1972, the 6-foot-8 giant was elected to the Basketball Hall of Fame.

Superstar Bob Pettit was not a "born athlete" like most professional players. He had to get along mostly on pride and a strong will. But by working hard, Pettit made a place for himself in the NBA. For 11 seasons, he was the power behind the Hawks of Milwaukee and St. Louis. When he left pro basketball in 1965, he had scored over 20,000 points. That was more than any other player had scored in NBA history.

Robert E. Lee Pettit, Jr., was born in Baton Rouge, Louisiana, in 1932. He was an only child, and his parents were quite wealthy. So Bob never suffered from the want of things, as did many children who became professional athletes. Even so, life was not always easy for young Bob Pettit.

When he started high school, Bob was 5 feet, 7 inches tall and weighed only 118 pounds. He got a place on the school's football team, but he was not a very good player. So after his first game, he was dropped from the team. Later that year, Bob

went out for baseball. Again, he was the first player to be cut from the team. Finally, in his sophomore year, Pettit tried out for the basketball team. But he didn't find a place there, either.

Many boys would have given up after all these letdowns. But Bob Pettit tried even harder. To improve his shooting, he made a basket out of a coat hanger and took shots at it with a tennis ball. When his father saw how much Bob wanted to play, he bought him a backboard, basket, and ball. With long hours of practice, Bob began to improve.

More than anything, Bob Pettit wanted to play on a team. So he and some other boys who had not made their high school teams started a church basketball league. With constant practice, Bob became the best player in the league. When he tried out for his high school team again in the fall, Pettit stood 6 feet, 4 inches tall. He had grown so much and improved so much in just one year that he easily made the team.

By his senior year, Pettit had grown to 6 feet, 7 inches. He led his team to 18 straight wins, and then to the 1949 state basketball championship. Bob's great playing won him a scholarship to Louisiana State University (LSU) in 1950. In his sophomore year there, he became the third-best scorer in the country. That wasn't good enough for Bob, though. He wanted to become the number-one scorer in the nation!

In his last year at LSU, Pettit almost made his goal. He and Frank Selvy of Furman University were about even in points, with each going into his last game. When Pettit scored 46 points against Georgia Tech, he thought the title was his. But when he opened the paper the next morning, he learned that Frank Selvy had won the title by scoring 100 points in his last game.

Bob had lost the title. But he had put up a good fight for it, making his last year at LSU a great one. Even so, many people did not think Pettit could make it in professional basketball. They said he was too skinny for the rough play in the pro game. But Bob Pettit did not agree. When people said he might not make it with the pros, it made him try that much harder. Pettit decided that he *would* make it as a pro—no matter what.

After he graduated in 1954, Bob signed with the Milwaukee Hawks of the NBA. Upon joining the team, Bob found that he would have to learn how to play basketball all over again. The team's coach wanted to use him at forward instead of at center— his usual position. This meant that Pettit could no longer play close to the basket and use his good

hook shot to score. But nothing kept Bob down for long. Before playing his first pro game, he worked on and perfected a jump shot that could not be stopped.

The Hawks built a new team around Pettit. After his first season with them, Bob left no doubt that he could play professional basketball. He averaged 20 points a game during the 1954-55 season, which made him the fourth-best scorer in the NBA. And when the season ended, he was named NBA Rookie of the Year!

In 1955, the Hawks moved from Milwaukee to St. Louis and were renamed the St. Louis Hawks. During the 1955-56 season, Bob Pettit established himself as a real superstar. He averaged 25 points a game that season, and won both the scoring and the rebounding titles. After the 1955-56 season ended, Pettit was named the NBA's Most Valuable Player. Bob had worked hard for this great award, and he could not have been prouder.

Bob Pettit's greatest moment of glory came two years later, at the end of the 1957-58 season. The St. Louis Hawks were playing the Boston Celtics for the NBA championship. The Hawks led the playoff series, three games to two. Then, in the sixth game, Pettit scored 50 points—including 19 of the last 21 his team got! As a result, Bob Pettit and the Hawks became the new world champions.

When Pettit retired from pro basketball in 1965, he took with him many records. He had been the first player in NBA history to score more than 20,000 points. (His 11-year total was 20,880, with an average of 26.4 points a game.) He had won two NBA scoring titles and two Most Valuable Player awards. In addition, he had led the Hawks to five NBA Western Division titles, and to the world championship of 1957-58.

But even more important was something that did not show up in the record books. And that was Pettit's desire and will to succeed. By having faith in himself, and by working hard, Bob Pettit had become one of the biggest of basketball's big men. In 1970, just five years after he retired, Pettit was elected to the Basketball Hall of Fame.

Bill Russell

Bill Russell helped make pro basketball the game it is today. He was not a high scorer, but he was one of the greatest defensive players of all time. Russell was the first player to make a practice of blocking shots. And he was one of the finest rebounders in NBA history. In the 13 years Russell played with the Boston Celtics, the team won 11 world championships. This record has never been broken. Without Bill Russell, it might never have been set.

William Felton Russell was born to a poor black family in Monroe, Louisiana, in 1934. When he was nine years old, his family moved to Oakland, California, in search of work. Bill's mother and father both found work in the Oakland shipyards during World War II. Then, after the war ended, Bill's mother became ill. She died a short time later, leaving Mr. Russell to raise Bill and his older brother, Charlie.

Charlie Russell was a star athlete in high school, and Bill wanted to be one, too. He tried out for football and baseball, but did not make either team. Then he tried out for basketball. Because he was taller than most boys his age, Bill made the team. But he was a poor shooter, and he scored only a few points. Luckily, though, the coach liked Bill enough to keep him on the team.

By his senior year, Bill Russell had grown to 6

feet, 5 inches. As a result, he was made the starting center for his team. He still did not score many points. But by blocking his opponents' shots, he showed himself to be a strong defensive player. So strong, in fact, that his team won the city title!

At the time, few people knew how important Bill Russell's defense had been to his team. Tall players were expected to be good shooters, and Bill's shooting had always been poor. So when he graduated from high school, only one college offered Russell a scholarship—the University of San Francisco. When USF asked him if he wanted to be the center on its basketball team, Russell said yes.

The USF Dons, as they were called, had never been a good team. And there was no reason to think that the new 6-foot, 9-inch center would change that. But he did. Bill Russell helped the Dons become a great defensive team. By blocking shots and by pulling down rebounds, he stopped other teams from scoring. As a result, the Dons needed only a few points to win. And win they did! In Russell's last two years with them, the Dons won 55 straight games. They also won two National Collegiate Athletic Association (NCAA) championships. Bill Russell was the man behind the wins, and everyone knew it.

When Russell graduated from college in 1956, he was one of the hottest players in basketball. The Harlem Globetrotters were ready to offer him $50,000 to play for them. Many NBA teams wanted him, too. But the team that wanted Russell the most was the Boston Celtics. The Celtics needed a big man who could pull down rebounds, and Russell fit the bill. Red Auerbach, the Celtics' coach, traded two players to the St. Louis Hawks for the right to sign him. Then Auerbach offered Russell a contract.

Bill wanted to play with the Celtics. But he did not sign with them right away. First he wanted to compete in the 1956 Olympic games, in Australia. After leading the U.S. basketball team to an Olympic victory, Russell returned home to America. Seven days later, he signed with the Boston Celtics.

The Celtics were already halfway through the 1956-57 season when Bill Russell joined them. Few people thought that he would make much of a difference to the team, coming so late in the season. But Russell proved that he *was* the difference— between a losing and a winning team. In the six years before Russell, the Boston Celtics had led the NBA in scoring, but they had never taken first place in the Eastern Division. And they had never won a world championship. Then Bill Russell joined the team. In his first season with the Celtics,

Bill Russell blocks as Oscar Robertson ("The Big O") reaches for the basket.

he led the team to *both* the Eastern Division title and the world championship of 1956-57!

The following season, Russell and the Celtics lost the NBA championship to Bob Pettit and the St. Louis Hawks. But one year later, in the 1958-59 playoffs, they won the title back. They did not lose it again until 1967! The Celtics' eight straight championships was an all-sport record. No other professional team had ever won eight world championships in a row. And the reason the Celtics won all those championships was a man named

Bill Russell. When other teams came up against Russell's powerful defense, they had to change their whole style of play. They could seldom shoot from close to the basket, for Russell would block those shots. Even when they got close enough for an easy jump shot, they had to loft it high because of Russell's long arms. Bill Russell was a master at blocking shots and at taking rebounds off the defensive backboards. As a result of his great defensive playing, he was named the NBA's Most Valuable Player *five times* between 1958 and 1965!

In 1966, coach Red Auerbach left the Celtics and retired from pro basketball. Bill Russell was signed as the team's player-coach for the next season. He thus became the first black man ever to coach a major league team in any sport. Unfortunately, the Celtics lost the 1966-67 Eastern Division playoffs. When this happened, many people blamed Russell. They said that he and the Celtics were too old and too tired. But Russell would not quit. He drove himself and the Celtics on to two more NBA championships—in 1968 and in 1969. Then, while he was at the top again, he retired from basketball.

The record books do not list all of Bill Russell's successes. Records are mostly for great scorers, and Bill averaged only 15 points a game during his career. But he was basketball's first great defensive player, and he changed the game as few others have. By blocking shots and by grabbing rebounds, he made other teams change their style of playing. Russell won no scoring titles, but he led the Boston Celtics to 11 world championships in 13 years. In addition, he won four NBA rebounding titles and five Most Valuable Player awards.

Bill Russell was pro basketball's greatest winner. But he was more than just a winner. At the end of the 1960s, he was voted the "greatest athlete of the decade." And in 1975, he was elected to the Basketball Hall of Fame.

Elgin Baylor

The world of professional sports has never seen anyone quite like Elgin Baylor. At 6 feet, 5 inches tall, he was not one of basketball's biggest men. He just seemed to be. The star of the Los Angeles Lakers attracted wide attention not only because of his skills, but also because of his great personality.

Elgin Baylor grew up in Washington, D.C., where he was born in 1934. He was always much taller than most boys his age, and he developed into a fine basketball player while still young. He was so good a player in high school that in 1954 he was the first black ever named to the all-city basketball team.

After high school, Elgin looked forward to playing basketball in college. Many colleges wanted Elgin to play for them. But Elgin's high school grades had been very poor, and few colleges could take a student with poor grades. Elgin ended up going to the College of Idaho on an athletic schol-

arship. After a year at Idaho, he won a scholarship to Seattle University (SU), a much larger college. Here, Elgin Baylor began his great career as a college player. In the 1956-57 season, he led his team to a record of 22 wins and 3 losses. The next season he led the team to the NCAA finals. Baylor was among the top three scorers in the country in both his seasons with Seattle.

During Baylor's years as a top college player, the Minneapolis Lakers had come upon hard times. They had not had a winning season since the great George Mikan had retired. In 1958, the Lakers drafted Elgin Baylor, hoping that he would make them a power again. Baylor did that and more. In his first pro season, he led the Lakers to a second-place finish in the Western Division of the NBA. Baylor and the Lakers made it all the way to the playoff finals, but they lost the NBA championship to the Boston Celtics. Even so, they had had a very good season.

Elgin Baylor was named NBA Rookie of the Year for the 1958-59 season. During his second season with the Lakers, he did even better. He averaged 29.6 points a game—second best in the NBA. And he set a new NBA record for points scored in a single game. While playing against the New York Knickerbockers in 1960, Baylor scored 71 points!

But Baylor did more for the Lakers than score points. It was just as important to make people want to come to the Lakers' games. And that is what Baylor did. He helped give basketball the excitement that fans were looking for. In this way, he kept the Minneapolis Lakers from going broke. When the team moved to Los Angeles in 1960, Baylor showed California what pro basketball was all about. Thousands of fans came to each of the Los Angeles Lakers' games just to see Elgin Baylor play. And he never let them down.

In only a few years, Elgin Baylor had become one of pro basketball's superstars. He also had become one of the best liked and most respected players in the game. No one thought more of him than the players on his team. From the start, Elgin was the leader of the Lakers—both on and off the court. Off the court, he became known for his fancy clothes and his sense of humor. If someone had a good story to tell, Elgin could always top it with an even better one. He could not be beaten in conversation, fancy clothes, card games . . . or almost anything else. Once, the Lakers took a vote on what color jackets the team should have. Blue was chosen by just one player: Elgin Baylor. But since Baylor was so highly thought of by his teammates, the team got blue blazers.

Elgin Baylor won the respect of his teammates by giving his all on the court. Many experts believe that he was the greatest forward who ever played the game. He used his strength to play rough. And he used the spring in his legs to go up over taller players for the rebounds. But most important was the way Baylor moved through the air before shooting. He seemed to hang in the air, twisting one way or the other, until he could shoot around the defensive players and make the basket. One newsman described Baylor's movement this way: "He has never really broken the law of gravity. But he is very slow about obeying it."

For all his skill, though, Elgin Baylor never played on a championship team. When Jerry West joined the Lakers, he and Elgin formed the greatest two-man scoring punch in the history of pro basketball. Even so, the Lakers failed to win even one NBA championship. They came close several times, but were beaten out by Bill Russell and the Boston Celtics.

Like so many hard-playing pros, Baylor fell victim to a number of injuries. In a 1965 playoff game against the Baltimore Bullets, he shattered his kneecap. Because of that injury and others, the next season did not go well for Elgin. He had his worst scoring average ever—16.6 points a game. He picked up his average to 26.6 points a game in the 1966-67 season. And over the next two years, he averaged about 24 points a game. But he never fully recovered from the injury to his kneecap.

Baylor retired from basketball in 1971. He left behind him a record of 23,149 points, and a career average of 27.4 points a game. Most basketball experts agree that Elgin Baylor was among the best all-around players in NBA history.

There are many places in America that are "basketball-crazy." In some parts of Ohio, it is said, parents give their babies basketballs to play with instead of rattles. One place where this might happen is Middletown, Ohio, where superstar Jerry Lucas was born in 1940. In Middletown, even the grade schools have organized basketball teams. Jerry Lucas was in the fourth grade when he started playing basketball. Except for one year after college, he has been playing the game ever since.

By the time he started high school, Jerry Lucas had developed into a very fine player. His Middletown team was almost unbeatable while he was on it. Jerry led the team to 76 straight wins and two state championships. When he was a senior, he and Middletown came close to winning their third title. But they were defeated in the semi-finals of the state tournament. With that, Middletown lost its chance for a third championship, and Jerry's high school basketball career came to an end.

But what a career it had been! Jerry Lucas had scored a total of 2,466 points, breaking the high school record set by the giant Wilt Chamberlain. Because of this, more than 100 colleges offered Lucas basketball scholarships. One school even included a high-paying job for Jerry's father in its offer. But Jerry turned down all the basketball scholarships. Instead, he chose to go to Ohio State University (OSU) on an academic scholarship. This scholarship was given to him because of his excellent grades in high school. (Jerry never said much about it, but he was as good a student as he was a basketball player.)

When Lucas got to Ohio State, he stood 6 feet, 8 inches tall and weighed 230 pounds. But he gave a lot more to the Ohio basketball team than just size. For one thing, he was a great shooter. Just as important, he was an unselfish player who would often pass to a teammate for a score rather than score himself.

Two of Lucas's teammates at Ohio were John Havlicek and Larry Siegfried, who both went on to become NBA stars. With such a fine team, Ohio State did very well. During Jerry's three varsity seasons, OSU won 78 games and lost only 6. The team ended the 1959-60 season with a bang, by winning the NCAA championship. After this big win, Jerry Lucas helped make a winner of the U.S. basketball team at the 1960 Olympic games. The U.S. team took the gold medal for first place, and Jerry took the honors as the team's leading scorer. Soon after the Olympic victory, Lucas was chosen as America's Sportsman of the Year.

By the time he graduated from OSU, Jerry Lucas was the most honored college player in basketball history. He had been named to the All-America team three years in a row. And twice, he had been chosen as College Player of the Year. In 1962, after winning all these honors, Lucas shocked the sports world. He said he did not want to play professional basketball! No one could believe it. But for a while, it looked as if Lucas really meant what he had said. He entered graduate school in 1962, and stayed there a year. For the first time since the fourth grade, superstar Jerry Lucas was out of basketball.

Lucas was not out for long, though. The Cincinnati Royals needed a strong player like Jerry, and they were determined to get him. He would give the Royals the size they needed. And teaming him with the great Oscar Robertson would give them enough power to challenge the Boston Celtics for the title. Finally, the Royals talked Jerry

45

Lucas into coming back to basketball.

Lucas played better than ever during his first year with the Cincinnati Royals. When the 1963-64 season ended, he was named NBA Rookie of the Year. Jerry followed this up by being named to the NBA's All-Star team for two years in a row. But he was unable to make the Cincinnati Royals a winning team. The Royals were good, but they were not good enough to make it to the NBA championship playoffs. When the 1968-69 season ended, Cincinnati traded Lucas to the San Francisco Warriors.

Jerry played with the Warriors for two years. Then, in 1971, he joined the New York Knickerbockers. The outstanding player almost lifted New York to the 1971-72 NBA title, but he didn't quite make it. When he and the Knicks went into the final playoffs against the Los Angeles Lakers, they were a crippled team. Even so, Lucas was determined to win. He kept the Knicks close to the Lakers with his great outside shooting. But Wilt Chamberlain and the Lakers outplayed him, and the Knicks lost the title in five games.

Jerry continued to play hard for the Knicks during the 1972-73 season. For the second year in a row, the Knicks made it to the NBA championship playoffs. This time, they won! Jerry Lucas did not play full time during the playoffs. But he was a valuable man to have on the court when he *did* play, and he helped the Knicks win the NBA championship.

Jerry is still with the New York Knicks. And though his best playing days are over, he remains an outstanding competitor. For excellence on and off the court, few basketball players are in a class with Jerry Lucas.

It will be a long time before anyone breaks all the basketball records set by Wilt Chamberlain. Wilt is not only the greatest scorer in NBA history, but also the greatest rebounder. Some people say he is the number-one basketball player of all time. If this is true, it puts Chamberlain above such other greats as George Mikan, Bill Russell, and Kareem Abdul-Jabbar!

Wilton Norman Chamberlain was born in 1936 in Philadelphia, Pennsylvania. By his sophomore year at Overbrook High School, he already stood 6 feet, 11 inches tall. Besides being tall, "Wilt the Stilt" was fast and strong. With all this going for him, Chamberlain decided to try out for basketball. He was an overnight star at the game. In the three years Chamberlain played for Overbrook, he led his team to a record of 58 wins and 3 losses. The team also won three Public League titles and two city championships. And it was mostly because of Wilt Chamberlain.

When Wilt graduated from Overbrook High in 1955, something remarkable happened. He was drafted by the Philadelphia Warriors of the NBA! The Warriors knew that Chamberlain would not be able to play pro basketball for four more years, but they were willing to wait for him. This was quite an honor for 18-year-old Wilt Chamberlain.

In the meantime, Chamberlain was offered scholarships by more than 200 colleges and universities. He chose to go to the University of Kansas. In his first two varsity seasons, Wilt averaged about 30 points a game. He led the Kansas team all the way to the NCAA championship playoffs in his junior year. But Kansas was defeated by the number-one college team in the country, North Carolina. Even though Wilt had played well, many people thought it was his fault that Kansas had lost the championship. They said he had not tried to win as hard as he should have—or could have.

Wilt Chamberlain knew this was not true. He had done his best on the court, but he had gotten little help from his teammates. Discouraged over the way things were going, Chamberlain left Kansas after his junior year. Wilt knew that because of NBA rules he would have to wait another year before turning pro and joining the Philadelphia Warriors. So he joined the Harlem Globetrotters, the world-famous team of black basketball stars. With Chamberlain on the team, the Globetrotters won 169 straight games!

Wilt played with the Harlem Globetrotters for one year. Then, in 1959, he signed a contract with the Philadelphia Warriors. Chamberlain was well known by then, and large crowds came to see him play. The 7-foot-2, 275-pound giant was so big and so good that other teams found it hard to stop him. All they could do was try to rough him up and hope that he did not score.

Chamberlain took a lot of physical punishment during his first year as a pro. But that did not stop him from setting four NBA records. These were for points scored in a single season (2,707), average points per game (37.6), rebounds grabbed in a single season (1,914), and average rebounds per game (28). At the end of the 1959-60 season, Wilt Chamberlain was named NBA Rookie of the Year. He was also named the NBA's Most Valuable Player!

Wilt Chamberlain had made basketball history, to be sure. But not everyone liked him. Whenever he scored a lot of points, his critics said he was selfish because he shot too much. And whenever he *did not* score a lot of points, his critics said he was not trying hard enough. Chamberlain and the

Philadelphia Warriors ended the 1959-60 season by losing the NBA championship playoffs to the Boston Celtics. After this happened, Wilt's critics blamed him for the loss. Chamberlain became so angry that he said he was going to retire. Luckily, though, he changed his mind.

During the 1960-61 season, Wilt broke both of his first-year scoring records. He scored over 3,000 points, averaging 38 points a game. In addition, he set a new one-game record for rebounds. He did this in November of 1960 when he grabbed 55 rebounds against the Boston Celtics. During the 1961-62 season, Chamberlain set a new NBA record for the most points scored in a single game. Wilt set this record in March of 1962 while playing against the New York Knickerbockers in Hershey, Pennsylvania. He made 36 field goals and 28 foul shots, for an unbelievable total of 100 points! By the end of the 1961-62 season, Chamberlain had scored 4,029 points, with an average of 50.4 points a game. These are scoring records that no other player has ever come close to matching, much less topping.

Wilt Chamberlain was setting one record after another. But, for the third year in a row, the Philadelphia Warriors lost the NBA title to the Boston Celtics. Again, Chamberlain was blamed for his

team's loss. Wilt's critics called him a "loser." They said that he cared more about setting records than he did about leading his team to victory.

In 1963, the Philadelphia Warriors were moved to San Francisco and renamed the San Francisco Warriors. Wilt played less than two seasons with San Francisco before being traded to the new Philadelphia 76ers. For the first time, Chamberlain was on a team that had a lot of top players. To prove that he was a good team player, Wilt spent much of his time blocking shots and passing to his high-scoring teammates. Wilt's scoring average

dropped, but he set new personal records for rebounds and assists. When the 1965-66 season
ended, Chamberlain was named the NBA's Most
Valuable Player.

Throughout the 1966-67 season, Chamberlain
concentrated on teamwork. He set no scoring
records that year. But he helped the 76ers set a
record of 68 wins and 13 losses—the best single
season in NBA history. Just as important, he
helped the 76ers end Boston's long string of championships. After defeating the Boston Celtics in the
Eastern Division playoffs, Chamberlain and his
team went on to defeat San Francisco in the championship playoffs. The Philadelphia 76ers won the
NBA title, and Wilt Chamberlain lost the tag of a
"loser." Nothing could have pleased him more!

Wilt made 702 assists during the 1967-68 season,
setting a new NBA record. When the season ended,
he was named the NBA's Most Valuable Player.
This was the *fourth time* Wilt had won this important award!

In 1968, Chamberlain was traded to the Los
Angeles Lakers. The team lost the 1968-69 NBA
title to the Boston Celtics. But two years later, in
the 1971-72 final playoffs, Wilt Chamberlain led
the Los Angeles Lakers to their first NBA championship. With two world championships and four

Most Valuable Player awards behind him, Chamberlain felt that he was ready to retire. So in 1973, basketball's greatest scorer and rebounder left the NBA.

Wilt Chamberlain remains the giant of basketball's giants. It will be a long time before all his records are broken. And it will be an even longer time before basketball sees another player like him.

The name of Willis Reed will not be found in pro basketball's record books. But if there were a record book for courage, Reed's name would surely be in it. In 1970, Reed led the New York Knickerbockers to a world championship that they could not have won without him. And he did it in spite of injuries and great pain.

Willis Reed grew up in Louisiana, where he was born in 1942. Always tall for his age, he was 6-feet-5 when he started high school. Willis was good at most sports, and he became an all-state football and basketball star. Of the two sports, basketball was Reed's favorite.

After he graduated from high school, Reed looked forward to playing basketball on the college level. Like many other top black athletes, he went to Grambling College in northern Louisiana. By this time, Willis was 6 feet, 10 inches tall and weighed 230 pounds. He was big enough and strong enough to have played on Grambling's well-known football team. But he played on the college's basketball team instead. As a freshman, Reed led his team to the national basketball championship for small colleges. And over the next three years, he helped Grambling win three Southwestern Conference titles in a row. When the high-scoring center was chosen to play in the 1963 Pan-American games, no one was surprised.

In 1964, after his great college career ended, Willis Reed set his sights on playing pro basketball. He was picked by the New York Knickerbockers in the second round of the NBA draft. But eight other college players were drafted before him, and Reed never got over this. Being a proud young man, he did not believe that there were eight other college players who were better than he was. So after he was drafted by the New York Knicks, Reed set out to prove that he was the best new player in the NBA.

Willis Reed put everything he had into his rookie season of 1964-65. Playing center for the Knicks, he averaged 20 points a game and was named NBA Rookie of the Year. The Knicks were proud of Reed, but they did not think they could win a championship with a 6-foot-10 center. So they drafted a bigger center, Walt Bellamy, and moved Reed to forward. Willis had trouble learning to play his new position, because he had always played at center. Finally, though, he adjusted to playing at forward.

After three more seasons, the Knicks still had not come close to winning a championship. So Walt Bellamy was traded, and Willis Reed was moved back to center — where he belonged. In time, Willis became the team leader of the Knicks. He also became one of New York's most popular athletes. The fans loved to watch him play, especially against giants like Wilt Chamberlain and Kareem Abdul-Jabbar. These players were much bigger than Reed, but they could not push him around. Once Reed took a position guarding the basket, *no one* could overpower him or push him away!

In 1969, after many years of false hopes, the Knicks at last put together a winning team. Willis Reed played better than ever, easily winning the NBA's Most Valuable Player award for the 1969-70 season. In spite of painful bone spurs, injured knees, and a bad hip, Reed led the Knicks to the Eastern Division title. Then, in the playoff series with the Milwaukee Bucks, Reed's great defensive play against Kareem Abdul-Jabbar carried New York to another victory. The Knicks, it seemed, could not be stopped.

The finals of the playoffs matched the New

York Knicks with the powerful Los Angeles Lakers. The Lakers' strongest player was its giant center, Wilt Chamberlain. Reed was four inches shorter, and he was playing on two bad legs that might fail at any time. Yet he battled Wilt on even terms until the fifth game of the series. Then, what the New York fans feared would happen, *did* happen. Willis Reed injured his hip and had to be taken out of the game. The Knicks won the fifth game. But, without Reed, they lost the next one.

The series was now tied at three games each. No one thought that New York could win the series without its big center, for no one else could hold down Chamberlain like Reed. Until a few moments before the start of the seventh game, no one knew whether Reed would be able to play. Reed *did* play—but only with the help of pain-killing shots before the game and again at halftime. He was unable to jump, and he could not run very fast. But he leaned on Chamberlain, using all his strength to keep Wilt away from the basket and the backboards. Reed scored only four points and grabbed only a few rebounds. But his presence on the court lifted the Knicks to victory. New York won the seventh game, 113 to 99, and became the new NBA champions.

For his great play and his even greater courage,

Willis Reed was voted the Most Valuable Player
in the NBA playoffs of 1969-70. After that season,
Reed's play had its ups and downs. Often, he
played only part time because of injuries. But in
1973, Reed shook off his injuries and helped the
New York Knicks win *another* NBA championship.
Again, he was voted the Most Valuable Player in
the playoffs.

Willis Reed may never achieve the recognition
he deserves among fans. That is because he does
not break records or make headlines. But the
proud Reed once said that he did not want to be

thought of as a "great player." He said that instead, he wanted to be known as a "man who gave 100 percent of himself" when he played. Those who saw Reed play in his first championship know that he gave even more.

The 6-foot, 7-inch forward Rick Barry has every right to be called a "superstar." Ever since he joined the NBA in 1965, he has been among pro basketball's top scorers. He has also been one of the game's most controversial players. In 1967, when Barry left the NBA and joined a rival league, he touched off one of the greatest legal battles in sports history.

Rick Barry was born in 1944 and grew up in Roselle Park, New Jersey. It was there that he learned to play basketball. Almost from the start, Rick was a player with a quick temper. But he did not let his temper get in the way of his shooting. He became his high school team's star player, scoring more points than anyone thought possible. As a result, Rick's team had one winning season after another.

When he graduated from high school, Rick Barry was offered basketball scholarships to over 30 schools. He chose to go to the University of Miami in Florida. In spite of his temper, which often got him into trouble, Rick became one of the leading scorers in the history of college basketball. During his last year at Miami, he averaged more than 37 points a game. When the varsity season ended, Barry was named the number-one scorer in the country.

Even though Rick had set new records in college basketball, many people did not think that he would make it in the pros. He was tall at 6-feet-7, but he only weighed 200 pounds. The experts said that such a skinny player would never be able to take the physical beating handed out by the giant pros. But, in spite of this, Rick was picked in the NBA's 1965 draft. The San Francisco Warriors had second pick of all the college players in the country, and they took a chance on Rick Barry.

Rick did not let the Warriors down. He took great punishment in his rookie season of 1965-66, but he did not back down from the battle. By averaging over 25 points a game, he proved himself to be a great shooter. Rick Barry was one of the few players who made the NBA's All-Star team. And when the 1965-66 season ended, the tall, skinny forward was named NBA Rookie of the Year. The "experts" were speechless!

To prove that his first-year success was no accident, Rick did even better the next season. Six times, he scored more than 50 points in a game. By raising his average to 35.6 points a game, he took the NBA scoring title away from Wilt Chamberlain. (No other player had done that in seven years!) Toward the end of the 1966-67 season, Rick Barry was again named to the NBA's All-Star team. He

scored 40 points in the rough All-Star game, and was named the game's Most Valuable Player.

After these two outstanding seasons with the San Francisco Warriors, Rick was known as one of the NBA's superstars. He was on the top of the basketball world. Then, in 1967, he got caught up in the most serious controversy of his career. The newly formed American Basketball Association

(ABA) had established a team in Oakland, California, just across the bay from San Francisco. The coach of the Oakland team was Bruce Hale, who was Rick Barry's father-in-law and his former coach at Miami. The ABA wanted Rick Barry to play for the Oakland Oaks, as the team was named. And Rick Barry wanted to play for Oakland's coach, Bruce Hale. So Barry left the Warriors and joined the Oaks, going from the NBA to the ABA. Then the battle began!

The ABA had tried to sign up many NBA players by offering them large sums of money. But Rick was the *only* NBA superstar who crossed over to the new league. He signed a contract with the Oakland Oaks for $75,000 a year. But the San Francisco Warriors said that Barry could not do this because he was still under contract to them. Before the start of the 1967-68 season, the Warriors went to court to stop Rick Barry from playing with the Oaks. The court ruled in favor of the Warriors, forcing Barry to sit out the entire 1967-68 season. He was not allowed to play with the Oakland Oaks, or with any other team in pro basketball. So for one year, Rick Barry worked as a sports broadcaster.

Late in 1968, Rick went back to the job he liked best—playing basketball. He played with the

Oakland Oaks, making them one of the finest teams in the ABA. The 6-foot-7, 215-pound forward scored 1,190 points in 35 games, for an average of 34 points a game. This won him the ABA's scoring title for the 1968-69 season. But more important, Rick's high scores helped the Oaks win the ABA championship.

In 1969, the Oaks were moved to Washington and renamed the Washington Capitols. Rick Barry led the team all the way to the ABA Western Division playoffs. The Capitols lost the playoffs in seven games. But, by averaging 40 points a game, Barry won the scoring title for the ABA playoffs. Later that year, he was named to the ABA's All-Star team. When the 1969-70 season ended, Rick's career average was 30.3 points a game. This was the highest career average in the ABA.

In 1970, when the Capitols were moved to Virginia, Rick asked to be traded to another team. And he was, to the New York Nets. He played with the Nets for two seasons. Then, in 1972, Rick's old legal battle with the San Francisco Warriors started up again. The courts ended the battle once and for all by saying that Rick Barry had been in the wrong. So Barry went back to the NBA and joined the team he had started with—the Warriors, renamed the Golden State Warriors. Having spent four years in the ABA, Rick Barry was once again a "rookie" in the NBA!

Rick is still with the Warriors, and he remains an excellent shooter. Through his years in both the NBA and the ABA, he has averaged more than 30 points a game. If he continues to score at that rate, Rick Barry will almost surely be included among the top two or three scorers in pro basketball history. As the record now stands, he is already one of the greatest forwards ever to pick up a basketball.

Kareem Abdul-Jabbar

Kareem Abdul-Jabbar, or Lew Alcindor, is one of the youngest superstars in professional basketball. But already, he is considered one of the greatest players in the game's history. Someday, he may be called the greatest basketball player of all time.

Jabbar was born Ferdinand Lewis Alcindor, Jr., in 1947. From the day of his birth, it was clear that he was going to be a big man. He weighed 13 pounds when he was born, and was more than 22 inches long! This was very big for a baby. But Lew's grandfather had stood 6 feet, 8 inches tall, and both of Lew's parents were above average in height. Most people were sure that Lew would be a tall man when he grew up. No one, however, dreamed that he would become a 7-foot, 2-inch giant!

Young Lew Alcindor was raised in New York City. When he entered grade school, he was already a head taller than his classmates. He was 6 feet tall when he started the sixth grade. And by

the time he reached the eighth grade, he was 6-feet-6, and still growing! Because of his remarkable size, Lew was offered an athletic scholarship to Power Memorial Academy, a Catholic high school with a good basketball team. Lew gladly accepted the offer.

When he entered Power Memorial, 13-year-old Lew Alcindor was 6 feet, 10 inches tall. He had the size and the desire to play basketball. But he was clumsy and awkward, partly because he had grown so fast. To help him with these problems, the basketball coach at Power put Lew on a special training program. He lifted weights to build up his strength, and he skipped rope to improve his coordination. After a lot of work and practice, Lew Alcindor became an outstanding basketball player. He was so tall and so agile that opposing players could not stop him from scoring. As a result, he made the Power Panthers an almost unbeatable team. The Panthers won 71 straight games between 1963 and 1965. They also won three high school championships in a row—first in 1963, and again in 1964 and 1965. Each of these years, Lew was his team's top scorer. And each year, he was voted the number-one player in the New York Catholic High School Athletic Association.

By the time he graduated, Lew Alcindor was

known throughout the basketball world. Almost every major college in the country wanted him. After thinking it over, Lew decided to attend the University of California at Los Angeles (UCLA). This decision came after a visit from Jackie Robinson, the first black man ever to play major league baseball. Robinson was a graduate of UCLA, and he talked Lew into going there.

When he arrived at UCLA in 1965, Lew Alcindor had reached his full height of 7-feet-2. He stopped growing, but he did not stop improving his basketball skills. During his first year at UCLA, Lew led the school's freshman team to a winning streak of 21 games. His scoring average for the year was 33 points a game. After he became a sophomore in 1966, Lew joined the UCLA varsity team, the Bruins. In his first game of the season, he scored a record-breaking 56 points. UCLA went on to win 30 straight games, as well as the NCAA championship of 1966-67. Lew, of course, was his team's top scorer, averaging almost 30 points a game.

Lew's second and third seasons of varsity play were much like his first. The giant center led the Bruins to two more NCAA titles, for a total of three championships in a row. In all, Lew Alcindor and the Bruins won 88 games out of 90 — a remarkable record. But it was not just Lew's great shooting that lifted his team to all those wins. Lew had become a fine defensive player as well as a great shooter. With his size, speed, and agility, he stopped other teams from getting near the basket and taking easy shots. As a result, few teams came even close to beating the UCLA Bruins.

Lew's skill on the basketball court made him a hero to millions. But few people knew anything about Lew Alcindor the man, or about his life off the court. Then, before he left UCLA, Lew did two very surprising things. First, he turned down an offer to play on the U.S. team at the Olympic games in Mexico City. The unselfish superstar did this so that he could spend some time working with children in poor black communities. A while later, Lew did something even more surprising. He became a member of the Muslim religion, whose founder was Muhammad. Lew had been studying the religion for a long time, and he liked its teachings. When he became a Muslim, Lew took the name Kareem Abdul-Jabbar. This was his Muslim name, and it was the name he wanted to be known by.

After Lew—now Kareem—graduated from UCLA, he was drafted by the Milwaukee Bucks of the NBA. He signed a five-year contract with them for over $1 million. In the 1969-70 season, his first with the Bucks, Kareem proved he was worth it.

He averaged 28.8 points a game, which made
him the second-highest scorer in the NBA. And he
helped the Bucks win 56 games, or twice as many
as they had won the year before. When the season
ended, Kareem Abdul-Jabbar was named NBA
Rookie of the Year.

During the 1970-71 season, Kareem became the
NBA's top scorer, averaging 32 points a game.
More important, he led the Milwaukee Bucks to
their first NBA championship. This great victory
came when Kareem and his team clobbered the
Baltimore Bullets in the playoff finals. Because of
his outstanding play, Jabbar was voted the NBA's

Most Valuable Player. He was only 24 years old when he received this top award.

Kareem won his second Most Valuable Player award at the end of the 1971-72 season. He also won his second scoring title that season, averaging 35 points a game. Two years later, at the end of the 1973-74 season, Jabbar was named the NBA's Most Valuable Player for the third time. He led the Milwaukee Bucks all the way to the NBA play-off finals that season. But he and the Bucks lost the championship to John Havlicek and the Boston Celtics. (This was Boston's 12th championship, and its first since Bill Russell retired in 1969.)

Kareem Abdul-Jabbar is still in the early years of his career. But he has already won three Most Valuable Player awards, along with several scoring titles and one world championship. Many basketball experts have said that Kareem is a combination of Wilt Chamberlain and Bill Russell. And just about all the experts agree that he is on his way to becoming the best basketball player of all time.

About the Author

Richard Rainbolt is a longtime sports fan who has written a number of lively, well-received sports books. Among them are *Gold Glory*, a history of the Minnesota Gophers; *The Goldy Shuffle*, the story of Bill Goldsworthy of the Minnesota North Stars; and *The Minnesota Vikings*, a fast-paced history of that famous team. As one might guess from his books, the author is a native of Minnesota. After serving in the U.S. Marines, Mr. Rainbolt attended the University of Minnesota, where he received a degree in journalism. Since then, he has worked as a newspaper reporter, a public relations man, and a reporter for the Associated Press. In addition to writing, Mr. Rainbolt now runs his own public relations firm.